MAKE IT, SHAKE IT, MiX iT UP

44 **Bible Stories** Brought to Life with **SCIENCE**

Nancy B. Kennedy

Illustrated by Jon Cannell

CONCORDIA PUBLISHING HOUSE • SAINT LOUIS

Published 2008 by Concordia Publishing House
3558 S. Jefferson Avenue
St. Louis, MO 63118-3968
1-800-325-3040 • www.cph.org

Illustrations © 2008 Concordia Publishing House

Text © 2008 Nancy B. Kennedy

Manufactured in the United States of America

1 2 3 4 5 6 7 8 9 10   17 16 15 14 13 12 11 10 09 08

For my parents,

James and Arleen Boyd,

who let us **explore**.

Contents

Part 2: New Testament Stories

Note to the Reader

The other day, my son squirted a half a tube of toothpaste into a glass of water. Now, usually that kind of youthful high spirits would have me thinking, "Isn't it time to release him back into the wild?" But not this time. This time I was thrilled! I laughed. I kissed him on the head. I encouraged him to swish it around and see what happens.

How else could I react when Evan, in all his 7-year-old earnestness, told me he was conducting a science experiment? For several years now, we've been in the kitchen conducting experiments of every imaginable kind. Our fun—and sometimes messy—activities resulted in my first book, *Even the Sound Waves Obey Him*, a collection of Bible stories and science activities for very young children.

Now, we're back in the kitchen again. *Make It, Shake It, Mix It Up* applies the same scientific approach for children in the upper elementary grades. The activities are a little more complex, requiring more materials in some cases and more steps in others. And, with many of the activities, children will have a chance to develop their waiting skills. But I'm confident they—and you— will have a good time. Many of the activities produce an object for your student or child to eat or keep; a gelatin snake, for example, or a crystal star. For children who want to explore further, I've added a section to some activities called "Try It," which contains suggestions for ways to make the activity more challenging.

Once again, I've tied each activity to a Bible story so the activities serve as a way to teach the timeless stories of our Christian faith. Each of the stories is followed by a brief and focused lesson, some very basic truth about God that students can take from the story and apply to their daily lives.

This time, I've added Bible memory verses to each story. They contain the words of God in Scripture or the words of someone who has encountered God. Encounters with both God and science are amazing—and very often mystifying. As you hear the reactions of people faced with the irrefutable presence of God, you become as awed as they undoubtedly were. Learning verses that record their thoughts and emotions—not to mention the very words of the living God—brings the Bible powerfully alive to anyone, child or adult.

Let me add a **word of caution** for teachers and parents. In this book, I've included some activities using materials that should be handled with caution. They are ordinary materials you have around the house or science room, things like rubbing alcohol, boiling water, knives, and bleach. Judge for yourself how capable your student or child is of handling these items and substances. If you are in any doubt, for safety's sake complete the steps using these things yourself.

I hope these activities whet your appetite for more scientific exploration, just as they did for Evan. Although his toothpaste-and-water experiment didn't make it into this book, one activity is to mix homemade toothpaste. I was dismayed when Evan wrinkled his nose at my concoction and refused to try it. Apparently, science doesn't appeal to all of his senses!

Nancy Kennedy

Part 1: Old Testament Stories

Images of God

Read It

Genesis 1–2:4

What do you do to feel good about yourself? Do you wear certain clothes? Do you act a certain way because you think it will help you make friends? It is tempting to try to be someone you're not so others will like you. But think about how God sees you. He made you in His image, to be holy like Him. But no one is perfect. No matter how hard you try, you can't make yourself holy. The good news is that even when you're not perfect, Jesus fixes you. Because Jesus died on the cross and took your sins upon Himself, you are restored to holiness. That means you don't need to try so hard to please other people or live up to your own unrealistic expectations. You already have God-given qualities that will please Him and allow you to be at peace with yourself. You can be confident because through Jesus, God values who you are.

Learn It

So God created man in His own image, in the image of God He created him; male and female He created them.

Genesis 1:27

Bubble Images

God captured His image in the creation of human beings. Let's capture images of bubbles on paper.

Do It

1. Pour bubble liquid into the small dishes, one for each color. To make your own, mix 6 parts water to 1 part dish detergent and 1 part glycerin (a skin care product found in drugstores) or liquid hand soap.

Get It

- Bubble liquid
- Water (optional)
- Dish detergent (optional)
- Glycerin or liquid hand soap (optional)
- Small dishes
- Tempera paints (liquid)
- Spoons
- Straws
- Bubble wands
- White construction paper

2. Squeeze a teaspoon of tempera paint into each dish and mix it in. Use one straw and one bubble wand for each dish to keep the colors from muddying.

3. Blow through a straw into one dish until the bubbles rise over the top of the dish, keeping your paper at hand. Remove your straw and quickly lower your paper onto the bubbles. Flip the paper over and pop any bubbles sticking to it. Repeat for each color.

4. To capture individual bubbles on the paper, blow bubbles through the bubble wand, let them land on the paper, and then pop them with your finger or another piece of paper.

Understand It

By popping your bubbles, you can capture their image on paper. If bubbles are left to pop on their own, they will slowly merge together and pop in one big blob of color. Bubbles merge because they always seek a shape having the least surface area, so the individual walls gradually break down.

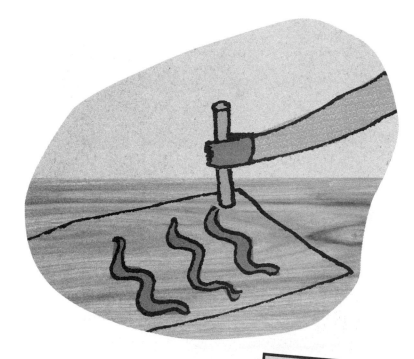

The Serpent Deceives

Straw Serpents

Satan disguised himself as a snake when he talked with Eve. Let's make slimy snakes of our own.

Do It

1. Empty four packets of gelatin powder into a bowl. Use any flavor you wish.

2. Carefully boil 2½ cups of water and pour it into the bowl. Depending on what color you want your snakes to be, add a few drops of food coloring. Whisk until the gelatin is dissolved, and let the mixture cool for a few minutes.

3. Set the straws up in an empty, clean juice or milk container or potato chip tube, using enough straws to fill it completely—you might need a hundred or more. (If you don't have enough straws, fill up any empty space with packing peanuts.) Plain straws work best, as the ridges of flexible straws tear the gelatin.

4. Pour the gelatin mixture into the straws and carefully set the carton in the refrigerator. Chill for 8 hours or until firm.

5. Tear the carton away from the straws and pull the straws apart. Starting from the empty ends, push the snakes out of the straws with your fingers onto waxed paper.

Understand It

Gelatin is a processed collagen taken from cow or pig bones, hooves, and connective tissues (yum!), combined with flavorings and colors. Boiled water breaks up the weak bonds of the gelatin's structure, and the powder dissolves. As the mixture cools, the structure begins to reform, but gaps occur in the process. Water is trapped inside these gaps, providing the jiggle that makes these snakes fun to eat.

Get It

- Flavored gelatin
- Large bowl
- Saucepan
- Water
- Measuring cups (optional)
- Food coloring (optional)
- Kitchen whisk
- Plastic drinking straws
- 1-quart juice or milk carton, or potato chip tube
- Waxed paper

Read It

Genesis 3:1–19

When you're thinking about doing something wrong—about sinning—you often have to talk yourself into it. You know it's wrong, but you're tempted to slip a toy into your pocket after playing at a friend's house. "He's got so many toys, he won't miss it," you think. "Besides, I'll get more fun out of it anyway." Eve knew God's rule—she told Satan right away what she wasn't supposed to do. But Satan got her to doubt what God said. It's often best to trust your first thought when you're tempted to sin. Satan is our enemy. Only Jesus can defeat him.

Learn It

[God said,] "I will put enmity between you and the woman, and between your offspring and her offspring; He shall bruise your head, and you shall bruise His heel."

Genesis 3:15

After the Flood

Read It

Genesis 6–9

After it rains, we may see a rainbow and stop for a moment to admire its beauty. We understand that a rainbow is formed when sunlight shines through droplets of rain or mist, but do we really see it for what it is—the sign of a promise from God to us? His promise was never again to destroy the earth and all living creatures by flood, even though He knew "the intention of man's heart is evil from his youth" (Genesis 8:21). Later, God chose another symbol, the cross, as a sign of an even greater promise to us. We have the promise of forgiveness through Jesus, who gave His life on the cross to take the punishment for the evil that we do.

Learn It

[God said,] "I have set my [rainbow] in the cloud, and it shall be a sign of the covenant between Me and the earth . . . . I will remember My covenant that is between Me and you and every living creature of all flesh. And the waters shall never again become a flood to destroy all flesh."

Genesis 9:13, 15

Rainbow Catcher

The rainbow is a fleeting symbol of God's promise. We can catch a rainbow on paper.

Get It

Black construction paper
Scissors
Bowl or pan
Water
Medicine dropper
Clear nail polish
Paper plate (optional)
Newspaper

Do It

1. Cut the construction paper into a shape that will fit into the bottom of your bowl or pan.
2. Pour at least an inch of water into the bowl. Press the paper under water to the bottom.
3. Fill the medicine dropper with a small amount of nail polish. If the neck of the bottle is narrow, pour some polish out onto a disposable plate to fill the medicine dropper.
4. Squeeze one drop of nail polish onto the surface of the water to form a "slick."
5. Lift the paper by the edges out of the water, catching the slick on the paper. Let the paper drip over the bowl, and then put it on a piece of newspaper to dry.
6. Hold it up to the light. What do you see?

Understand It

White light, which reflects off of everything we see, is composed of waves that have many different wavelengths, which our eyes see as different colors. The nail polish bends, or refracts, the white light shining on it. Because the nail polish slick varies in thickness, the light is refracted in different ways, producing colorful patterns. You can see the same thing when light reflects off of a soap bubble or a puddle of gasoline on a wet street.

Moving Flip Book

Once God told Abraham to get going, he was on the move. You can create the illusion of action from pictures that don't really move.

Do It

Get It

Notepad

Colored pencils

Stencil (optional)

Stamps and ink pad (optional)

1. Use a notepad in which the sheets of paper are attached at one end either by adhesive or spiral binding. If you are using loose paper or card stock, secure the pages at one end using a hole punch and fasteners or string.

2. Think of a scene you wish to draw, one that has movement and perhaps color changes. Beginning on the first sheet of paper, draw the first scene. On the second page, draw the same scene but with slight changes in the objects' position on the page.

3. Continue through the notepad, drawing 20 or more repetitions of the scene with its changes. For example, you could draw a sunset over a hillside with a bird flying overhead and a hiker walking by. Or, you could draw simple geometric shapes rolling or falling, or use a stencil or stamps and an ink pad.

4. When you're done, hold the notepad in one hand where the pages are secured and riffle the pages with your other hand. What do you see?

Understand It

Scientists think our eyes take up to forty "snapshots" each second and send them to our brain. Between the snapshots, our brain fills in the gaps, making some guesses about how the objects in the snapshot might move. That's why we see the action in a movie or on television—or in your flipbook—as continuous movement, although we actually are seeing a series of still pictures.

Abraham on the Move

Read It

Genesis 12:1–9

Abraham was a very rich man—he had gold and silver, cattle and flocks of sheep. He had a large and loving family. He was comfortable and happy where he lived and had grown up. Yet when God told him to go to a place he had never seen, faithful Abraham packed up everything and got moving. On his way, he faced famine, war, and family sorrows, but he never turned back. God had promised to make a great nation from his family—the nation out of which the Savior would come—and Abraham believed Him. He remained faithful, and he worshiped God along the way. And God kept His promise to Abraham.

Learn It

[The Lord said,] "And I will make of you a great nation, and I will bless you and make your name great, so that you will be a blessing. I will bless those who bless you, and him who dishonors you I will curse, and in you all the families of the earth shall be blessed."

Genesis 12:2–3

Abraham beneath the Stars

Read It

Genesis 15

It never hurts to ask a question! Just ask Abraham. God assured Abraham that he would be safe and have his reward. Abraham believed Him but wanted to know more—he wanted to know why God hadn't blessed him with children. So he asked. God answered Abraham with the information that his family would be huge, too many even to count. Abraham wanted to know even more! How could he be sure God would keep His promise? God answered him with a dream. God might not give you an answer as specific as Abraham's, but He wants you to ask in faith. You can pray with confidence. Just like Abraham trusted God, you can also trust God because He keeps His promises.

Learn It

And [God] brought [Abraham] outside and said, "Look toward heaven, and number the stars, if you are able to number them." Then He said to him, "So shall your offspring be." And he believed the LORD, and He counted it to him as righteousness.

Genesis 15:5–6

Crystal Stars

When Abraham looked up into the sky, he couldn't count the number of stars he saw, just as God said he wouldn't be able to count his descendants. Let's make one of those shining stars.

Do It

1. Cut a chenille wire into three equal pieces. Twist one piece around another piece in the middle, and then tie the third piece around the other two to make a 6-armed star. Or, come up with your own design—you can use string as part of the star too. The star should fit into the jar without touching the sides. Cut to fit if necessary.

2. Attach the star to the middle of a pencil, tying one end of a piece of string, or twisting a twist tie, to one arm of the star and the other end to the pencil. The string or twist tie should be long enough to allow the star to hang into the jar without touching the bottom. Set the star aside.

3. Boil 2 cups of water and pour it into the jar.

4. Measure ¼ cup of borax and add it a spoonful at a time to the water, stirring to dissolve. Some undissolved powder may settle at the bottom of the jar.

5. Lower the star into the jar, resting the pencil on the rim. Set the jar in an undisturbed place for 24 hours. Lift the pencil. What do you see?

Understand It

Borax contains boron, a naturally occurring mineral that has been refined and allowed to crystallize. When the water is heated, its molecules move apart and make room for the borax crystals to dissolve. As the solution cools, the water molecules move back together, squeezing out the borax. As the water releases the excess borax, crystals begin to form on your stars.

Get It

- Chenille wires
- Scissors
- Pint jar (wide mouth)
- Pencil
- String or twist tie
- Saucepan
- Water
- Measuring cups
- Borax powder
- Spoon

Salt Sculptures

Lot's wife ended her life as a pillar of salt. With a little time, we can make sculptures from table salt.

Do It

1. Cut six lengths of string, each about six inches long. Knot them together at one end.

2. Bring 1 cup of water to a roiling boil on a stovetop in the pan. Add a few drops of food coloring, if desired.

3. Gradually add ¼ to ½ cup of salt, stirring constantly so it dissolves.

4. When no more salt will dissolve, take the pan off the burner. (You might see a film of salt crystals forming on the surface at this point.)

5. Place your jar in an out-of-the-way place where it will not be disturbed. (To protect the surface below it, put the jar on a saucer or place it on newspaper.) Pour the salt water solution into the jar. Submerge the knotted end of your strings into the solution and dangle the strings over the rim of the jar at even intervals.

6. After a few days, take a look at your strings. What do you see?

Get It

- Scissors
- String
- Saucepan
- Water
- Food coloring (optional)
- Measuring cup
- Salt
- Spoon
- Jar
- Saucer or newspaper

Try It!

Make this a long-term project. Add more salt solution whenever the water level drops below the knot. Add different colors of salt water and see what kind of sculpture you can "grow" over time.

Understand It

Sodium chloride, or salt, has a crystal structure. Salt dissolves in water until the point at which the solution is called saturated. Heat allows more salt to dissolve. But as the salt water begins to cool, the water cannot contain as much salt. The salt molecules that are squeezed out begin to re-form into crystals on your jar and string.

Lot's Wife Looks Back

Read It

Genesis 19:1–29; Luke 17:32–33

When you disobey your parents, you suffer consequences. Perhaps they take away privileges or forbid outings with friends. God's angels told Lot and his wife not to look back on the burning cities of Sodom and Gomorrah. Yet Lot's wife did look back, and God punished her. Perhaps she longed for her comfortable life in that evil place and was sad that God had destroyed her home and possessions. We aren't told why God took her life. We only know that she was warned, she chose to disobey, and the consequences were severe and permanent. Our disobedience—called sin—resulted in a permanent consequence too: Jesus' death on the cross. Jesus suffered for every sin ever committed, but the result was something good for us: forgiveness and the promise of eternal life.

Learn It

[Jesus said to the disciples,] "Remember Lot's wife. Whoever seeks to preserve his life will lose it, but whoever loses his life will keep it."

Luke 17:32–33

It's History

Visitors to the 700-year-old Wieliczka Salt Mine near Krakow, Poland, can see towering sculptures and blazing chandeliers made entirely from salt crystals.

The Life of Jacob

Read It

Genesis 28:1–22, 50

God kept His covenant with Abraham by blessing his family: first through his son, Isaac, and then his grandson Jacob. Each of them believed God when He said He would make them a great nation. Yet these men and their families were very human—they quarreled, they lied, they tricked each other, they were selfish. In fact, they were no different from families today! Yet God chose this family to bring His blessing on the world, the blessing of Christ's redeeming work of salvation from sin, and He kept His promise. You can believe God when He makes a promise to you.

Learn It

And God said to him, "I am God Almighty: be fruitful and multiply. A nation and a company of nations shall come from you, and kings shall come from your own body. The land that I gave to Abraham and Isaac I will give to you, and I will give the land to your offspring after you."

Genesis 35:11–12

It's History

In ancient times, Egyptians used natron, a naturally-occurring salt found along the banks of the Nile River, to embalm bodies and preserve them as mummies. Earlier Egyptians simply buried bodies in the desert, where the heat and sand accomplished the same process.

Apple Mummies

At his death, Jacob was embalmed, which is a way of preserving a body. Let's preserve apples in a similar way.

Get It

Plastic baggie (quart size)
Measuring cup
Salt
Baking soda
Powdered bleach, washing soda, or kitchen cleanser
Knife
Apple
Craft stick

Do It

1. In the baggie, add ¼ cup of salt, ½ cup of baking soda, and ½ cup of washing soda, powdered all-fabric bleach, or kitchen cleanser. Close the bag and shake to mix.

2. Cut an apple in half lengthwise through the core. With the craft stick, carve a face into an apple half. Push the stick into the apple, as you would to make a candied apple.

3. Plunge the apple half into the dry mix, making sure the apple is covered.

4. Check on your apple over the next week. What happens to it?

Understand It

You've made a mummy! The solution of sodium chloride (salt), sodium carbonate (washing soda), and sodium bicarbonate (baking soda) draws moisture out of the apple over time while preserving its shape and preventing mold from growing.

Cabbage Colors

God made Moses' hand white with leprosy, then healthy again. We can change the color of cabbage-tinted water using household substances.

Do It

1. Cut a quarter of a red cabbage into small pieces and put it in a wide-bottomed bowl. Pour ½ cup of boiling or very hot tap water over the cabbage. Cover and let it sit for about 15 minutes.

2. Spread a large piece of waxed paper out on a table. Put a piece of white paper under the waxed paper if the table is not white or light colored. (Waxed cereal bags also work.)

3. Pour the cabbage juice into another bowl and discard the cabbage leaves. The juice should be purple.

4. Using a medicine dropper, make several puddles of cabbage juice on the waxed paper.

5. Into each puddle, add a different substance—lemon juice, vinegar, ammonia, or a pinch of baking soda. (Clean the dropper thoroughly after each use, or use separate droppers for each substance.) What happens?

Understand It

The color of red cabbage comes from a pigment called a flavonoid. Because of this, red cabbage is what's called an indicator: you can change its color by changing its acidity. Acids (vinegar, lemon juice) turn the juice pink. Bases (baking soda, ammonia) turn the juice green.

Get It

- Red cabbage
- Knife
- Bowls
- Measuring cup
- Water
- Waxed paper
- Medicine droppers
- Lemon juice
- White vinegar
- Ammonia
- Baking soda
- White paper (optional)

Try It!

Try other foods, household cleaners, crushed aspirin, or other substances. For an extra challenge, add an acid to one puddle then add a base to the same puddle. You can return the juice to its neutral state.

Read It

Exodus 3–4:17

Unlike faithful Abraham, Moses questioned God out of a lack of faith. God chose Moses to lead His people, the Israelites, out of slavery in Egypt and into the land of Canaan as He had promised. Yet Moses protested God's calling, not believing that God would equip him with the abilities he needed for the task. All of God's signs—a burning bush, a shepherd's staff suddenly becoming a snake, a healthy hand turned white with leprosy—failed to move Moses forward into faith. God became angry with him (Exodus 4:14). God gave Moses signs as proof that Moses could trust Him. God sends us signs as well. These signs are recorded in His Word, the Holy Bible. When we are baptized, the Holy Spirit gives us the gift of faith to believe that God's Word is true. By reading God's Word, you can move forward in faith.

Learn It

Then the LORD said to him, "Who has made man's mouth? Who makes him mute, or deaf, or seeing, or blind? Is it not I, the LORD? Now therefore go, and I will be with your mouth and teach you what you shall speak."

Exodus 4:11–12

Across the Red Sea

Read It

Exodus 13:17–15:20

God works in our lives so He will be glorified (Exodus 14:4). That's what happened here on the banks of the Red Sea. Upon seeing the Egyptian army, the Israelites' first reaction was to panic, and then to question God's plan for them. Despite their many proofs of God's love for them and His continuing protection of them, this time they believed that God was nowhere to be seen. Yet God can accomplish the impossible. The Israelites were saved but the enemy was washed away. Jesus does the same thing. With His Word and through Baptism, He washes away our sins and offers us forgiveness and grace. Trust that God has plans to bring glory to Himself through your life, even when you feel lost or afraid. Then you can praise God as the Israelites finally did.

Learn It

Then Moses and the people of Israel sang this song to the LORD, saying, "The LORD is my strength and my song, and He has become my salvation; this is my God, and I will praise Him, my father's God, and I will exalt Him."

Exodus 15:1–2

Pillar of Cloud

The Israelites couldn't see God at work, even though He was visible as a pillar of cloud during the day and a pillar of fire at night. Let's make a pillar of cloud that we can see.

Do It

1. Drape the garbage bag or construction paper over the lunch box to create a dark background. (Black kitchen appliances work as a background too.)

2. Fill the bottle with about 2 inches of very hot (but not boiling) water. Quickly cap the bottle. Shake the bottle for a few seconds and set it on the table.

3. Working close to the bottle, light the match and let it burn for a few seconds. Uncap the bottle and drop in the match. Quickly cap the bottle again.

4. Lay the bottle on its side and press as hard as you can on the bottle for 10 seconds. Release and repeat a few times. Use potholders if the bottle is too hot to touch.

5. Pick up the bottle and unscrew the cap. Squeeze the bottle in front of your dark background. What do you see?

Get It

Water

Plastic bottle with cap (1- or 2-liter size)

Match

Potholders (optional)

Black plastic garbage bag or construction paper

Lunch box

Understand It

You've made a cloud! Clouds form when invisible water vapor in the air condenses into visible water droplets or ice crystals. The hot water in your bottle created a vapor in the air to which the smoke particles from the burned match could cling. By pressing down on the bottle, you lowered the air pressure inside the bottle and cooled the water, forming a cloud that you could see when it puffed out of the bottle.

Reflecting God's Glory

Mirror Writing

God wants us to reflect His glory. Let's see how the reflections of mirrors can sometimes be disorienting.

Do It

1. On a 3 × 5 card, write your name or a short phrase in a way that you think can be read correctly in a mirror.

2. Hold the card up to the mirror. Can you read it?

3. Now, holding a new 3 × 5 card up to your forehead, look in the mirror. As you look in the mirror, write the same words so they can be read in the mirror.

4. Compare the two cards. How did you do?

Understand It

We see objects in a mirror because it is hit by particles of light, called photons, and then reflects those photons back to us. A mirror is smooth, so the light is not scattered but reflected straight back, producing a clear image. Plane mirrors such as these reflect a reverse image: if you raise your right hand, your image will raise its left hand.

Get It

3 × 5 cards

Pencil or marker

Wall mirror and hand mirror

Try It!

For a challenge, place a hand mirror to the side of a 3 x 5 card placed on a desk in front of you. Looking into the mirror, try to write on the card so it can be read in the mirror.

Read It

Exodus 34; 2 Corinthians 3:7–18

A mirror gives you a pretty good idea of what you look like, whether or not you like what you see! When Moses was given the Ten Commandments—God's covenant with His people—his face shone as brightly as a mirror, reflecting God's glory to those around him. Think about who—or what—other people see in you. Do they see a dim reflection of what you're trying to be without God's help—the popular kid, the super-athlete, or the academic star—or do they see a reflection of God in you? We share in the glory of God through the new covenant of Jesus Christ. We become more like Jesus through His work in our life.

Learn It

Yes, to this day whenever Moses is read a veil lies over their hearts. But when one turns to the Lord, the veil is removed. Now the Lord is the Spirit, and where the Spirit of the Lord is, there is freedom. And we all, with unveiled face, beholding the glory of the Lord, are being transformed into the same image from one degree of glory to another.

2 Corinthians 3:15–18

It's History

Leonardo da Vinci, the fifteenth-century artist of Mona Lisa fame, used mirror writing in his notebooks, beginning at the right side of the page and moving to the left. Try writing a sentence in cursive, as Leonardo did, starting at the right. (If you have trouble, try using both hands, writing backward with your usual hand while writing forward with the other hand.)

Wandering in the Wilderness

Read It

Numbers 13–14

If you've ever been bullied, you know what it's like to have an enemy. The children of Israel were bullied by the Egyptians. But after Pharaoh let them go, they also turned to sinful ways. Their sin made them enemies of God. It's sad that the Israelites had to find out what having God as an enemy was like. Because of their rebellion, He caused them to spend forty hard years wandering in the desert before they finally arrived at the rich land God had promised them. We are sinful, just like the Israelites were. This makes us enemies of God as well. How do we become His friends again? Through Jesus, of course. Jesus made it possible for us to be forgiven because He took the punishment for our sinful ways.

Learn It

"According to the number of the days in which you spied out the land, forty days, a year for each day, you shall bear your [sins] forty years, and you shall know My displeasure." I, the LORD, have spoken.

Numbers 14:34–35

Try It!

Try this activity using colored craft sand on white paper. (You can make your own by shaking a few drops of food coloring with sand or salt in a zip-top bag. Let it dry before using.) Brush a layer of glue on the paper and then make your paths. Let the paper dry before you pick it up.

Salt Paths

The Israelites wandered in the wilderness for forty years. Let's make wandering paths etched in salt.

Do It

1. Set your ruler or dowel over the edge of a tabletop or counter. Hold it in place with a few phone books. (A narrow folding wooden ruler works well.)

2. Make a funnel with the card stock. Using the overturned cereal bowl, trace a circle in the card stock and cut it out. Cut out one quarter of the circle (a wedge shape) and draw in the edges of the remaining circle to form a funnel. Tape it together, leaving a ¼-inch hole at the base.

3. Punch out three equally spaced holes around the rim of the funnel. Cut three pieces of string and knot one end of each to the ruler and the other end through each of the three holes. The tip of the funnel should be suspended about one inch off the ground.

4. Place a large square of dark-colored construction paper under the funnel. Block the tip of the funnel with one finger and fill the funnel with salt.

5. Gently push the funnel in a circular motion while you remove your finger from the funnel. Follow the wandering salt!

Understand It

Your pendulum moves in predictable paths based on a principle called simple harmonic motion. The salt makes circular paths as the pendulum swings, gradually losing energy as friction slows it down.

Get It

- Ruler or dowel
- Phone books
- Card stock
- Cereal bowl
- Pencil
- Scissors
- Tape
- Hole punch
- String
- Dark construction paper
- Salt

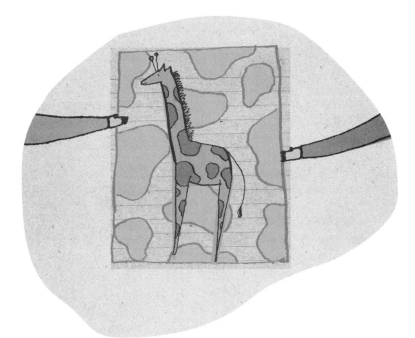

Camouflage Artists

Spies often use camouflage to disguise themselves. Let's see how God uses camouflage in nature for the protection of animals.

Get It

Black construction paper or colored card stock

Correction fluid or markers

Colored pencils

Scissors

Do It

1. Use one piece of construction paper or card stock as a backdrop. Dot it randomly with correction fluid or marker.

2. From another piece of paper or card stock of the same color, cut an animal shape. Draw it by hand or use a pattern you have at home or can find on the Internet.

3. On one side of the animal, draw the face, legs, tails, fins, or whatever is appropriate for that animal. Dot the other side with the same color correction fluid or marker as the backdrop you've made.

4. Have a friend hold your animal, face side out, against the backdrop. Easy to see, right?

5. Now, close your eyes and have your friend turn the animal over to the dotted side and hold it up, or attach it with a loop of tape, to the backdrop. Open your eyes. Is it still easy to see?

Understand It

Fish, animals, insects, and other creatures often use camouflage for protection from predators. Their coloring, texture, or shape makes them look like their environment. Desert animals, for example, often are a sandy color. A squirrel is not only the earthy color of trees and ground, but its fur is also rough and uneven to mimic tree bark. The exoskeletons of walking stick insects make them look like sticks, leaves, and leaf stems—they can even sway on their legs as if blown by a breeze.

Read It

Joshua 2

After Moses died, Joshua became the leader of the people of Israel. It was his job to take them into the Promised Land. Because people already were living there—enemies of God's people—Joshua wanted to see what he was up against. So he sent spies ahead. To blend in, these spies may have dressed like the people in Jericho. They were spotted, though, and made a harrowing escape. God protected the spies through a woman who gave them the information they needed—that people in Jericho knew God was with the Israelites and that the Israelites would conquer the land. This Bible story teaches us that God is faithful to His children and provides protection as they journey to the Promised Land. For God's children today, the journey to the Promised Land is our life in this world as we look forward to life in heaven.

Learn It

[The Lord said to Joshua,] "Have I not commanded you? Be strong and courageous. Do not be frightened, and do not be dismayed, for the LORD your God is with you wherever you go."

Joshua 1:9

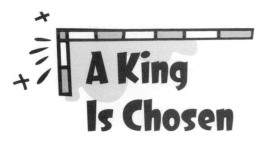

A King Is Chosen

Read It

1 Samuel 16:1–13

How much time do you spend looking in a mirror? Be truthful! But God does not consider what we look like—our shell—to be important at all. Samuel thought Jesse's son Eliab looked like a king. He might have been tall or handsome, a real charmer. But God chose young David because he was "a man after My heart" (Acts 13:22). To God, that meant David would do what God asked of him. Let's think about that. What does a child of God look like? Can you tell by looking at someone whether he or she is a child of God? Probably not. What does it mean to be after God's heart? In truth, none of us is after God's heart. Sometimes we do things that displease God. Yet through the work of the Holy Spirit, God chooses us as His loved and redeemed children. The next time you see yourself in a mirror, smile and show your joy that you are chosen!

Learn It

[The Lord said to Samuel,] "The LORD sees not as man sees: man looks on the outward appearance, but the LORD looks on the heart."

1 Samuel 16:7

Eggs-actly!

If our "shells" aren't important to God, let's stop worrying about them! We can use an egg to demonstrate how God values our inner being.

Do It

1. Carefully place the egg in the container so the shell doesn't crack.

2. Pour enough vinegar into the container to cover the egg.

3. Put the lid on the jar and let it sit for 24 hours. Observe it at intervals. What happens?

Understand It

The vinegar—which is acetic acid—reacts with the eggshell, which is made of calcium carbonate. The reaction causes carbon dioxide bubbles to form on the shell, which then dissolves completely over time. The egg remains intact because it is protected by a thin membrane inside the shell. If you're careful, you can pick up the egg without breaking it.

Get It

Jar with a lid

Raw egg

White vinegar

Try It!

For more fun, cover the egg with corn syrup. Over time, water molecules from inside the egg migrate through the porous membrane into the syrup, leaving the egg flabby. This process is called osmosis. To plump up the egg again, remove it from the syrup and put it in water. Water molecules will migrate back into the egg, firming it up again.

Milk Glue

David and Jonathan had a friendship that was stronger than glue. Did you know that milk can be made into a truly sticky glue?

Do It

1. In a bowl, mix 2 tablespoons of powdered milk into ¼ cup of hot water until it dissolves.

2. Pour 1 tablespoon of vinegar into the bowl. Stir until the mixture separates into solid curd and watery whey.

3. Place a strainer over a cup and line it with a coffee filter. Pour the mixture into the filter. Drain off the liquid. Take out the curd and pat it dry on a paper towel.

4. Put the curd back into the bowl and chop it up with a spoon. Add 1 teaspoon hot water and ¼ teaspoon baking soda. Mix until the substance smoothes out. Add more water or baking soda to make a thick liquid or paste. (The foaming you may see is carbon dioxide gas from the reaction between baking soda and vinegar.)

5. Try your glue. Paste together paper, cardboard, foam shapes—anything you'd normally glue together. Let it dry. How does it work?

Get It

- Bowl
- Powdered milk
- Measuring cups and spoons
- Water
- Vinegar
- Spoon
- Strainer
- Coffee filter
- Cup
- Paper towel
- Baking soda

Understand It

Your glue is the result of two chemical reactions. First, the acidic vinegar sours the milk, separating it into solid curd and liquid whey. Second, the baking soda neutralizes the acid in the mixture. The milk curd is composed of a protein called casein, a substance that acts as an adhesive.

Read It

1 Samuel 18–20; Proverbs 18:24

The bond of friendship between David and Jonathan was unbreakable. The two young men proved themselves as friends many times over. As heir to the throne, Jonathan could have considered David a rival and joined his father, Saul, in his attempts to kill David. After David became an enemy in Saul's eyes, he could have deserted Jonathan to protect his life. But each man made a vow of friendship, considering it a promise to God (1 Samuel 20:8). Now read John 15:12–16 to see what Jesus says about friends. Our best Friend, Jesus, showed His love for us by dying on the cross for our sins. You can show your love for your friends by valuing them as gifts from God.

Learn It

A man of many companions may come to ruin, but there is a Friend who sticks closer than a brother.

Proverbs 18:24

God's Law Uncovered

Read It

2 Kings 22

Most of the kings in the history of Israel and Judah—the two kingdoms of the once united Israel—were evil. But Josiah, the king of Judah, was obedient to God and aware of his nation's moral decay. Yet when he found the Book of the Law, he was stricken with remorse. Even as a good king, he realized how far short he and his people came of obeying God's Law. Josiah ended idol worship in the temple and tore down altars built to honor false gods and practice immoral religions. The example of Josiah can teach us that one of the purposes of God's Law is to show us our sin. When we read God's Word, we learn which of our actions, words, and thoughts are disobedient to God's will. Knowing that, we should repent, which means recognizing and regretting our sins, confessing them to God and changing our actions.

Learn It

[The Lord said,] "Because your heart was penitent, and you humbled yourself before the LORD, when you heard how I spoke . . . you have torn your clothes and wept before Me, I also have heard you, declares the LORD."

2 Kings 22:19

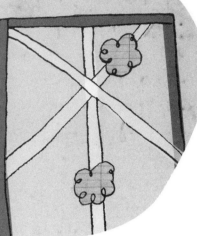

Spiderwebs

When Josiah finally uncovered the book of God's Law, perhaps it was covered in dust and spiderwebs. Let's play a game to see how spiderwebs work.

Do It

1. Crisscross a doorway with tape, with the sticky side of the tape facing you, to make a spider web. Stick the tape ends to either side of the doorway.

2. Using more tape, mark lines on the floor at 4 feet, 5 feet, 6 feet, and 7 feet from the doorway.

3. Allot 2 or more cotton balls to each player. To add weight to the cotton balls, glue a small button to each cotton ball. Or make loops with tape and stick two cotton balls together.

4. Form teams and start at the 4-foot mark. Throw cotton balls at the web, trying to get as many as possible to stick. Award points for every success, and play in rounds, moving back for each round.

Get It

Wide masking or packing tape

Cotton balls

Glue

Small buttons

Understand It

Spiders spin webs from a liquid silk that is released through tubes called spinnerets inside their bodies. The silk can be stronger than steel! Insects get stuck in the sticky strands of the web, causing vibrations that alert the spider to a possible meal. Some strands of the web are not sticky, allowing the spider to walk along it freely. And some spiders have a kind of oil on their feet that prevents them from sticking to their own web. How many "insects" hit their mark in your game?

Sparkle Art

We can make a sparkly painting that would have looked right at home in Esther's palace. Salt and water do the trick!

Get It

- Measuring cups and spoons
- Water
- Small containers
- Food coloring
- Salt
- Art brushes
- Construction paper

Do It

1. Pour ¼ cup of water into each container. Add a few drops of food coloring to each container to make as many colors as you want.

2. Into each container, add 1 tablespoon of salt.

3. Using a brush, swish the salt around and paint your design on a piece of construction paper. (Light-colored paper works best.) Each time you dip your brush in the water, swish the salt around so your brush picks up a lot of it.

4. With the help of an adult, preheat an oven to its lowest setting. Carefully place the paper in the oven and set a timer for 10 minutes.

5. When the paper is dry, take it out. Glittery art!

Understand It

As your painting dries, the water evaporates, which is the process of a liquid changing into a gas. (Liquid and gas are two states of matter; solid is another.) The salt is left behind. As it dries, the salt forms into crystals with flat sides that reflect light, making them sparkle.

Read It

Esther 3–4

Esther's life sparkled! She was beautiful. She was a queen. She wore royal robes and a crown. She had maids to dress her and care for her. She won the favor of all who saw her (Esther 2:15). Yet God did not intend for her to live a life of luxury for her own enjoyment. He chose Esther to preserve the Jewish nation in preparation for the coming of Jesus as the Messiah. She may not have even been aware of her exact role in history. Yet she was willing to die for her people. God accomplished His will through Esther. And He accomplishes His will through you!

Learn It

[Mordecai told them to reply to Esther,] "If you keep silent at this time, relief and deliverance will rise for the Jews from another place, but you and your father's house will perish. And who knows whether you have not come to the kingdom for such a time as this?"

Esther 4:14

The Trials of Job

Read It

Job 1–2, 38–42

When you make something of your own design, you take pride in it. You show your painting or your building-block robot to your mom or dad and maybe display it in your room. God taught one man, Job, that He and He alone created everything. Job was suffering—read the whole Book of Job to see how badly—yet his suffering allowed him to understand God better as his Creator and as the Creator of all we see and know. Like Job, we can take pleasure in God's handiwork, just as the Bible says the angels did at the dawn of creation.

Learn It

"Who then is he who can stand before Me? Who has first given to Me, that I should repay him? Whatever is under the whole heaven is Mine."

Job 41:10–11

Try It!

Make a belt from a manila folder. Cut off the tab so you have a straight edge and use the existing fold. Mark 45 lines at ¼-inch intervals and cut as directed before. (After every few cuts, you might want to cut the fold. It's difficult to reassemble the folder to cut the fold all at once.) How many people does this amazing belt fit around?

3 × 5 Card Belt

We can't create anything on our own. We can only work with what God has created. Let's change a small card into something else.

Get It

3 × 5 card
Pencil
Ruler
Scissors

Do It

1. Fold the 3 × 5 card lengthwise.

2. Mark nineteen lines across the long side of the card at ¼-inch intervals.

3. Starting at one end, cut from the fold to the open end on the first line, stopping ¼ inch from the edge.

4. On the second line, cut from the open end to the fold, stopping ¼ inch from the edge. Alternate cutting the lines starting from the fold and the open end until you reach the other end, which should be a cut from the fold.

5. Starting at the first line, cut the fold until you get to the last line, leaving ¼ inch of the card uncut on each end.

6. Open out the card. Is it big enough to wear?

Understand It

You can slip the card over your head and around your waist. By cutting the card, you changed its shape and size. The world is made up of what scientists call matter—in the form of liquids, solids, and gases—and matter can change. Scientists observe matter and how it changes by using the five senses—sight, hearing, smell, taste, and touch.

Solomon's Seasons

Green Time

Solomon says we cannot see the whole scope of God's work from beginning to end. From looking at a green leaf in the summer, we can't tell what it will look like in the fall, but a little rubbing alcohol can help us.

Do It

1. Collect green leaves from at least three deciduous trees (oak, maple, etc.).

2. Tear or cut the leaves into small pieces and pack them into separate jars for each leaf type. Label the jars with masking tape.

3. Cover the leaves with rubbing alcohol and mash the leaves into the alcohol with a plastic knife. Put lids on the jars.

4. Place the jars into a shallow baking pan and pour in about an inch of hot tap water. Swirl the jars every 5 or 10 minutes and replace the water in the pan as it cools with hot water. (Use a turkey baster to remove the cold water, or remove the jars and empty the pan.)

5. Once the alcohol has become dark green, remove the jars from the water and take off the lids. Cut thin strips of coffee filter paper. Place one end of the strip in the alcohol, and drape the other end over the top of the jar. Label the loose end with the leaf type and secure with tape.

6. Let the filters sit in the jars for 60 to 90 minutes. What do you see?

Get It

- Green tree leaves
- Small jars with lids
- Masking tape
- Pen
- Rubbing alcohol
- Plastic knives
- Shallow pan
- Water
- Turkey baster (optional)
- Coffee filter
- Scissors

Understand It

Through photosynthesis, plants use the sun's energy to produce the fuel it needs to grow. Leaf pigments play an important role by reflecting light. A chemical called chlorophyll gives plants their green color. The gold, yellow, orange, or red pigments you see on the filter are carotenes and xanthophylls that are usually hidden until fall, when chlorophyll breaks down. A chromatogram, which you've just made, reveals these colors. Because of differing chemical properties, the pigments travel up the coffee filter at different rates, making distinct lines on the paper.

Note: Avoid inhaling the alcohol fumes directly.

Read It

Ecclesiastes 3:1–11

We usually plan our day based on outcomes we know. You leave for school in the morning and arrive home in the afternoon. You go to the park, but you're back in time for dinner. You do your homework before bedtime. But Solomon says that we don't really know God's entire plan for us from beginning to end. He has planned experiences for us to enjoy—or to endure—and the timing of those experiences is up to God. Like Solomon, we can rest in the knowledge that God has plans for us. We can thank Him for the good days, and rely on Him for help with the bad days. And we can be certain that God's plan is for us to one day live with Him in heaven.

Learn It

For everything there is a season, and a time for every matter under heaven. . . . He has made everything beautiful in its time. Also, He has put eternity into man's heart, yet so that he cannot find out what God has done from the beginning to the end.

Ecclesiastes 3:1, 11

Ezekiel Eats God's Message

Read It

Ezekiel 2–3:11

The people of Israel were exiles in Babylon because of their sin and hard-heartedness toward God. In the Book of Ezekiel, we learn how God called one young man, Ezekiel, to be His spokesman to them. God tells him what to say to the people of Israel, and the message is not good: the people of God would have to endure hardship and persecution. But when Ezekiel eats the scroll that God gives him—a paper covered with words of sorrow and sayings of doom—he says it tastes as sweet as honey to him. Through the prophet Ezekiel, we are assured that God is in control. Therefore, when you recognize God's claim on your life, no matter what it means for you, God's calling will be sweet.

Learn It

"Son of man, all my words that I shall speak to you receive in your heart, and hear with your ears. And go to the exiles, to your people, and speak to them and say to them, 'Thus says the Lord GOD.' "

Ezekiel 3:10–11

Frozen Treat

God's scroll tasted as sweet as honey to Ezekiel. Today, that would be like saying it was as sweet as another treat we all enjoy—ice cream!

Do It

1. Pour ½ cup of cream, ½ teaspoon of vanilla, and 1 tablespoon of sugar into one of the quart size bags. Press as much air as possible out of the bag and zip it closed.

2. Put the bag into the other quart size bag. (Double-bagging helps prevent leakage.) Place the double-bag inside the gallon size bag.

3. Fill the gallon bag with 4 cups of crushed ice (two trays of ice) and pour ¼ cup of salt over the ice and the inner bags. Press the remaining air from the bag and zip it closed.

4. Wrap the bag with a towel or put on gloves (that ice is cold!) and begin to shake and squish the bag, making sure the ice surrounds the cream mixture.

5. Get out your spoons!

Understand It

In order to melt, ice has to absorb energy. When you use ice to cool the milk mixture, the energy comes from the ingredients and from your warm hands. Salt lowers the freezing point of water, so even more energy has to be absorbed for the ice to melt. This makes the ice cold enough to freeze the ingredients into ice cream.

Get It

Measuring cups and spoons
Heavy cream
Vanilla extract
Sugar
Plastic freezer zipper bags (gallon and quart size)
Ice
Salt
Towel or gloves
Iced tea spoons
Coffee can (optional)
Peanut butter jar (optional)

Try It!

If you don't mind a racket, you can also do this activity with a plastic peanut butter jar inside of a coffee can (with lids on both). Roll it around forcefully on a floor, along hallways, or down ramps—whatever space you have!

Invisible Ink

In this event, God gave Daniel the ability to "read" the king's dream. You and a friend can read each other's thoughts, even if they're written in invisible ink!

Do It

1. Wet your paper lightly with a spray bottle and let it dry. (You don't have to do this step—this simply wrinkles the paper, disguising the writing.)

2. Put one spoonful of baking soda into the container. Add ½ cup of water and stir to mix. Dip your brush or swab into the mixture and write your message. Let the paper dry.

3. Hand your secret message to a friend. Dip a clean brush or cotton swab into the grape juice and brush it across the page, covering it. Can you read your message?

Understand It

Grape juice contains an acid that reacts with the baking soda, which is sodium bicarbonate, a base that reacts with acids. Because of the chemical reaction, a different color appears wherever the secret message is written.

Get It

- Spray bottle
- Water
- White paper
- Spoon
- Baking soda
- Small containers or bowls
- Measuring cups
- Art brushes or cotton swabs
- Purple grape juice

Read It

Daniel 2

If you woke up one morning and asked a friend to tell you what you dreamed about overnight and what the dream meant, could your friend do it? Hardly! Yet that was what King Nebuchadnezzar was asking others to do for him. The dream itself was a doozy! (Read the rest of the chapter for the dazzling details.) Deciding what a dream like that meant would be hard enough. But who can really know what another person is dreaming or even thinking? God gave Daniel the special gift of interpreting Nebuchadnezzar's dreams. Daniel's prophecies were about the grace of God and the coming Messiah. God gives each of us special gifts. The most important is the gift of faith, which comes to us through God's Word and through the sacraments of Holy Baptism and the Lord's Supper.

Learn It

Daniel answered and said: "Blessed be the name of God forever and ever, to whom belong wisdom and might. . . . He reveals deep and hidden things; He knows what is in the darkness, and the light dwells with Him."

Daniel 2:20, 22

A Mysterious Message

Read It

Daniel 5

Has anything ever scared you so badly that your knees knocked together and your legs gave way, as King Belshazzar's did? Fingers writing on a wall, as described in this Bible story, would certainly do it! God gave Daniel the ability to decode the mysterious writing. Although the message was bad for the Babylonian king—the end of his kingdom—he must have realized the justice of God's judgment on his godless ways. Rather than blaming the messenger, the king honored Daniel. Just as God sent Daniel as a messenger to King Belshazzar, God sends messengers to us today. Pastors deliver God's Word in sermons and teach us the meaning of Bible stories. God cares how you live your life, so He sends pastors, among other believers, to teach and guide you.

Learn It

[Daniel said,] "You have praised the gods which do not see or hear or know, but the God in whose hand is your breath, and whose are all your ways, you have not honored." **Daniel 5:23**

It's History

In ancient Greece, the Spartan army used a similar device to convey military messages. Called a scytale (pronounced skee-ta-lee), it was a wooden cylinder around which the sender wrapped a strip of parchment or leather and wrote his message. The strip was unwound and carried to the recipient, who rewound it and read the message.

Secret Code

Once again, Daniel interprets a message from God for a king. You can send a message to a friend without anyone else knowing what it says.

Do It

1. Cut 1-inch wide strips of paper or adding machine paper. If using paper, tape the ends of the strips together to form one long strip.

2. Tape one end of the strip to the cylinder of the rolling pin or paper towel roll at the left end, so it hangs down toward the floor.

3. Wind the strip around the rolling pin to form a spiral with the edges of the strip just touching until you get to the other end. Cut off any excess paper and tape the strip at the other end.

4. Write your secret message along the length of the rolling pin, left to right, placing one letter on each strip, beginning a new row each time you reach the end of the pin.

5. When you finish, unwrap the paper from the rolling pin. Can you read the message now?

Understand It

You've just created a cryptograph—meaning "hidden writing" in Greek—a device for enciphering and deciphering text. To read the message, your recipient needs to rewind the strip around a cylinder of the same diameter. Diameter is measured by holding a ruler up to center of the cylinder's end and noting the distance in inches or centimeters.

Get It

Scissors
Ruler
Adding machine paper or strips of paper
Tape
Rolling pin or paper towel roll
Pencil, marker, or crayon

Tight Squeeze

God caused a great fish to swallow Jonah, keeping him alive in the sea and delivering him to dry land. We can make a bottle swallow an egg and then spit it back out again.

Do It

1. Fill one of the containers with very hot water. (Add some boiling water, if you feel it is safe to do so.) Fill the other with cold water. Add ice cubes to the cold water so it is really cold.

2. Choose a glass bottle with a neck that is slightly smaller than your egg.

3. Put the bottle in the hot water for 5 minutes. Take it out and immediately put it in the cold water. Wet the egg and put it point down on the bottle top. What happens?

Understand It

When the air inside the bottle is heated, it expands, meaning that its molecules spread out. That increases the air pressure inside the bottle. As the ice water cools the air in the bottle, the air molecules contract, or move closer together, and the air pressure inside the bottle decreases. Now, the air pressure outside the bottle is greater, so it pushes the egg into the bottle.

Get It

- 2 large containers
- Water
- Ice cubes
- Glass bottle
- Hard-boiled egg, shelled

Try It!

To get the egg out, simply put the bottle back in the hot water. It squeezes out!

Read It

Jonah 1–4

Unlike Ezekiel, who immediately answered God's call, Jonah did not welcome God's call when it meant going to Nineveh, a city of evil people. Perhaps Jonah was frightened or wanted the Ninevites to experience God's judgment rather than His mercy. Jonah tried to avoid the work God wanted him to do by running away. But God did not let Jonah off so easily. The lives of a great many people, from the sailors on the ship at sea to the entire city of Nineveh, depended on Jonah answering God's call. The Lord spared Jonah's life and gave him a second chance. Jonah preached to the Ninevites and they were spared God's anger. Even then, Jonah did not understand the full extent of God's mercy (Jonah 4). We don't always understand it either. But we are all called to pray for all people and to rejoice when they turn to God.

Learn It

[Jonah prayed,] "Those who pay regard to vain idols forsake their hope of steadfast love. But I with the voice of thanksgiving will sacrifice to You; what I have vowed I will pay. Salvation belongs to the LORD!"

Jonah 2:8–9

Part 2: New Testament Stories

God's Light on Earth

Read It

Luke 1:5–25, 57–80

Cell phones, instant messaging, text messaging, online chat rooms, e-mail—we love to talk! What if you couldn't talk for nine entire months? God took away Zechariah's voice because he was slow to believe God's promise of a son who would prepare the way for the Messiah. During those months of silence, Zechariah had time to think about what the angel Gabriel told him. When God allowed him to speak again, Zechariah told others exactly what the angel had told him—that his son, John, would proclaim the coming of Christ. His time of silence was well spent. Perhaps God wants to speak to you. Give silence a try!

Learn It

[Zechariah prophesied, saying,] "Because of the tender mercy of our God, whereby the sunrise shall visit us from on high to give light to those who sit in darkness and in the shadow of death, to guide our feet into the way of peace."

Luke 1:78–79

Light Surprise

Zechariah called Jesus "the sunrise" that gives light (Luke 1:78). We can make light without plugging anything in or turning anything on.

Do It

Get It
Balloon
Fluorescent light bulb
Wool sweater

1. In a darkened room, inflate a balloon and tie it.

2. Hold a fluorescent bulb in one hand with the contact point facing out.

3. With the other hand, rub the balloon on a wool sweater for 15 seconds.

4. Touch the balloon to the bulb contact. What happens?

Understand It

It lights up! To light a fluorescent bulb, a mercury vapor is activated, carrying an electrical current across an arc and activating phosphor, the white coating on the inside of the bulb that emits light. Even the smallest amount of electricity applied to the electrode of the bulb can start the process. That's why you could power it using the static electricity from your balloon.

Gelatin Mounds

Blessings upon blessings were mounded upon Mary for her belief. Let's mound gelatin grains using static electricity.

Do It

1. Blow up a balloon and tie it.
2. Pour the gelatin out onto a paper plate.
3. Rub the balloon on a piece of wool for 15 seconds.
4. Bring the balloon down on top of the gelatin, almost touching it. Slowly lift the balloon.
5. What happens to the gelatin?

Get It

- Balloon
- Unflavored gelatin
- Paper plate
- Wool fabric

Understand It

The gelatin mounds into long, skinny stalagmites! Rubbing the balloon on wool charges it with static electricity, which is an imbalance of positive and negative charges. A balloon, like all matter, has atoms with charged and neutral bits. It becomes negatively charged when it is rubbed against wool. When the charged balloon is brought near the gelatin, the gelatin's negative bits are repelled by the negatively charged balloon. With its positive bits now closest to the balloon, the gelatin jumps up to meet it. See how tall you can make your stalagmites!

Read It

Luke 1:26–56

That a poor, unmarried girl would have a baby could hardly be called a blessing in Bible times. It would have meant hardship and scorn, a bleak future with no hope. Yet Mary humbly accepted her blessing, trusting in God although she didn't know what it would mean for her. "I am the servant of the Lord," she said; "let it be to me according to Your word" (Luke 1:38). Upon visiting her cousin Elizabeth, who would soon be the mother of John the Baptist, she became excited about her future, praising God and rejoicing in the coming Messiah. We can't know what the future on this earth means for us, but we can be certain that our future in the world to come is God's promise to us. Just as He fulfilled His promise to send the Savior, God keeps His promise to forgive our sins and provide salvation through our Savior.

Learn It

And Mary said, "My soul magnifies the Lord, and my spirit rejoices in God my Savior, for He has looked on the humble estate of His servant. For behold, from now on all generations will call me blessed; for He who is mighty has done great things for me, and holy is His name. And His mercy is for those who fear Him from generation to generation."

Luke 1:46–50

Angels Proclaim Jesus

Read It

Luke 2:8–19

We can create many barriers to believing God's simple messages and promises to us. If, instead of appearing to lowly shepherds that night, the angels had appeared to the more educated members of society, or the more wealthy, or the more religious, perhaps these people wouldn't have found it so easy to believe that the Messiah had just been born, and born in a stable at that. When we rely on our own abilities, we can become too educated, too wealthy, or too religious in the wrong way to humbly receive God's simple offer of salvation alone through Christ, the sleeping Babe in the manger. God leads us to this message—the miraculous means of salvation—by providing us with His Word, the Bible, and then giving us pastors, teachers, parents, and other believers to follow.

Learn It

And the angel said to them, "Fear not, for behold, I bring you good news of a great joy that will be for all the people. For unto you is born this day in the city of David a Savior, who is Christ the Lord."

Luke 2:10–11

String Telephone

Wouldn't a telephone have made the announcement of Christ's birth easier? Let's see how a piece of string and a cup can carry a message just like a telephone.

Get It

String
Ruler
Scissors
Plastic cups
Paper clips

Try It!

Make a "party line" by crossing two lines in the middle and creating four receivers.

Do It

1. Cut 12 or more feet of string, perhaps enough to reach into two rooms.

2. Using scissors or another sharp object—be careful!—punch a small hole in the bottoms of two plastic drinking cups.

3. Thread one end of the string from the outside into one of the cups, and then do the same with the other end and cup. Tie a knot in each end around a paper clip inside each cup. (A paper clip should be resting against the inside bottom of each cup, with the string between.)

4. Holding one cup, have a friend take one cup and move away from you until the string is pulled tight. Hold your cup up to your ear while your friend talks into his or her cup. What do you hear?

Understand It

When your friend talks into the cup, you should be able to hear what he or she says! Your friend's voice creates sound waves that cause the bottom of his or her cup to vibrate rapidly. The vibrations travel through the stretched string and into your cup, making it vibrate too. The sound waves travel into your ear, where you receive your friend's message via your "telephone."

Cola Bomb

Both Simeon and Anna exploded with praise upon meeting the baby Jesus. Here's an explosion you'll love—just be sure to set this up outside!

Get It

Diet cola (2-liter bottle)

Mentos® candy (1 roll)

3 × 5 cards

Clear tape

Do It

1. Set a bottle of warm soda on a flat surface, such as a bench, a sidewalk, or a driveway out-of-doors.

2. Tape together two 3 × 5 cards on a long end, both front and back, overlapping ¼ inch to create a 5 × 5¾ inch card. Roll the card up starting at one of the 5¾-inch sides. Tape it closed.

3. Cover the bottom of the tube with another 3 × 5 card and drop in the candies. Your tube should hold a dozen candies.

4. Working quickly with a partner, unscrew the cap of the bottle. Set your tube onto the mouth of the bottle, remove the card and let the candies drop all at once into the soda. Quickly remove the tube and step back!

Understand It

Believe it or not, this reaction is not a chemical one. It's a physical reaction that demonstrates the surface tension of liquids. At the surface, the molecules of the soda form a strong bond, despite the presence of the bubbles, which are created by pumping carbon dioxide into the liquid. Both the candy's microscopically pitted surface and its oily candy coating create a massive infusion of new gas bubbles, breaking the surface tension of the soda and causing the geyser-like explosion.

Read It

Luke 2:21–40

Angels announced the coming of the Messiah to many people: Mary, Joseph, Zechariah, and the shepherds. But God told people in other ways too. As an unborn baby, John the Baptist leaped at Mary's presence. The Holy Spirit told Simeon he would see the Messiah, just as He allowed Elizabeth to recognize Mary's baby. Perhaps as a prophet, Anna heard about Jesus directly from God. A star announced Jesus' birth to the Wise Men and guided them to Bethlehem. God spoke to them in a dream afterward, as He had spoken to Joseph in a dream. Today God speaks to us through His Word as it is preached to us in church and as we read it on our own. We respond the same way that Simeon, Anna, and the shepherds did: with our thanks and praise. In fact, we may say the very same words Simeon did in our worship services today!

Learn It

[Simeon said,] "Lord, now You are letting Your servant depart in peace, according to Your Word; for my eyes have seen Your salvation that You have prepared in the presence of all peoples, a light for revelation to the Gentiles, and for glory to Your people Israel."

Luke 2:29–32

John the Baptist's Message

Read It

Mark 1:1–8

John the Baptist could have enjoyed a comfortable life as the beloved only son of Elizabeth and Zechariah. Instead, he left his home to live in the wilderness. He wore simple clothes and ate plain food. When the time for his ministry came, he willingly accepted his mission as Jesus' herald and preached repentance and Baptism. Hundreds of years earlier, the prophet Isaiah predicted that John would prepare the way for Jesus (Isaiah 40:3), and John himself said: "A person cannot receive even one thing unless it is given him from heaven" (John 3:27). What was the result of John's work? Those who listened to John readily recognized Jesus as the promised Messiah. We are blessed when we know what God wants us to do, and we do it.

Learn It

And [John the Baptist] preached, saying, "After me comes He who is mightier than I, the strap of whose sandals I am not worthy to stoop down and untie. I have baptized you with water, but He will baptize you with the Holy Spirit."

Mark 1:7–8

Homemade Toothpaste

Should you brush after eating wild honey and locusts? Here's how to make toothpaste, just in case.

Do It

1. Crush six antacid tablets in the bowl with a spoon.

2. Add 1 tablespoon of baking soda, ½ teaspoon of water, and 1 teaspoon of glycerin. Mix until you have a smooth paste. Add more of any ingredient to smooth it. (If you don't have antacid tablets, you can substitute 1 teaspoon of salt.)

3. Add a small drop of flavored oil or extract, such as peppermint or wintergreen mint.

4. Brush your teeth! What do you think?

Understand It

Most toothpastes contain fluoride (to prevent cavities), a cleaning agent, an abrasive mineral, a foaming agent, and flavoring. Your toothpaste has calcium carbonate (the antacid tablets), which is the abrasive mineral, and sodium bicarbonate (baking soda) for cleaning. The glycerin smoothes the texture, while your flavoring adds taste. But because your toothpaste has no fluoride and most antacid tablets contain sugar, it would not be an exact substitute for commercial toothpaste.

Get It

- Bowl
- Spoon
- Antacid tablets
- Measuring spoons
- Baking soda
- Water
- Glycerin
- Flavored oil or extract
- Toothbrush
- Aluminum foil (optional)
- Damp cloth (optional)
- White cloth (optional)

Try It!

To test the abrasive quality of your toothpaste, put a dab of toothpaste on the shiny side of a strip of aluminum foil and rub it for about 15 seconds. Wipe the foil with a damp cloth and then dry it. Has its shininess worn off? You can check your toothpaste's cleaning power too. Rub a colored substance on white cloth—jam or coffee, for example. Let it dry. Rub your toothpaste over the stain. Does it lessen or get rid of the stain altogether?

The Holy Spirit Rests on Jesus

Descending Drops

At Jesus' Baptism, the Holy Spirit descended like a dove. What happens when drops of water fall from a floating ice cube?

Get It

Clear jar
Cooking oil
Ice cube

Do It

1. Pour cooking oil into a clear jar until it is about 3/4 full.

2. Drop an ice cube into the oil. Where does it end up?

3. Watch the ice cube. What happens to it?

Understand It

The density of a substance can change depending on its temperature. An ice cube, which is water in its frozen state, is less dense than oil, so it floats on top. But water in its liquid form is more dense. As the ice cube melts, the drops of water fall down to the bottom of the jar. When the ice cube melts entirely, you have a layer of water under the layer of oil.

Read It

Matthew 3:5–17; John 1:29–34

John the Baptist was quick to tell people that he wasn't worthy even to be a servant to the coming Messiah. So when Jesus came to be baptized by John—an act that held great significance—John was reluctant to do it. Later, however, John acknowledged that God used this Baptism as a way to point him to the Messiah. As Jesus' cousin, John knew Jesus by sight, but God gave him this beautiful visual sign, the Holy Spirit descending as a dove, that the long-awaited Messiah stood before him. The Trinity was clearly present here—in Jesus, in the Holy Spirit taking the form of a dove, and in the voice of God. The same is true when we are baptized in the name of the Father, Son, and Holy Spirit. Through this Sacrament, our sins are washed away once and for all.

Learn It

[John the Baptist said,] "He who sent me to baptize with water said to me, 'He on whom you see the Spirit descend and remain, this is He who baptizes with the Holy Spirit.' And I have seen and have borne witness that this is the Son of God."

John 1:33–34

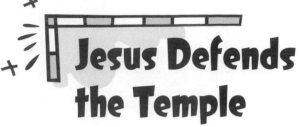

Jesus Defends the Temple

Read It

John 2:13–25; Psalm 69:9

How do you imagine Jesus? As the loving Shepherd who cares for His sheep? As the kindly Savior who beckons young children to come? Until now, Jesus had performed just one miracle, one that had helped a family avoid disgrace by changing water into wine at a wedding in Cana. But here, the disciples see another side to Jesus. He angrily drives out greedy people who are using the temple, a place of prayer and worship, for their own profit. Yet this is a true picture of Jesus too. He cannot allow people to disgrace God's name or His Church. Jesus is both loving and holy. Read verse 19. What temple was Jesus referring to in this verse? Not the physical temple. Jesus allowed His enemies to crucify Him, yet three days later He rose again, proving that He has power over all evil and death.

Learn It

For zeal for Your house has consumed me, and the reproaches of those who reproach You have fallen on me.

Psalm 69:9

Pinhole Camera

Jesus overturned the tables of people who were misusing the temple. We can turn the world upside down with a homemade camera.

Get It

Potato chip tube with lid
Ruler
Pencil or marker
Scissors or knife
Packing tape
Aluminum foil
Thumbtack

Do It

1. Remove the lid from the potato chip tube. Mark a line around the tube, about two inches from the bottom. Using scissors or a knife, cut around the line so your tube is in two pieces.

2. Fasten the plastic lid on the cut side of the smaller piece. Reassemble the container with the lid on the inside of the can. Tape the two pieces together with the larger piece on top.

3. Roll the container in aluminum foil and tape the foil in place. (This is to darken the tube.) Fold the extra foil over the top of the tube so the opening is narrowed to a small circle. This will darken the end you look through.

4. With the thumbtack, punch a hole in the center of the bottom of the tube, opposite the end with the folded foil.

5. On a sunny day, go outside and put the tube up to your eye, with the pinhole pointed out. Put both you and the objects you look at in the sun. (For best results, stand with the sun behind you.) What do you see?

Understand It

You've just made a camera! A pinhole camera is a type of *camera obscura*, a Latin term for "dark chamber." The pinhole allows you to isolate a single image, and the way light reflects off the image makes it appear upside-down on your plastic lid or waxed paper screen. Some photographers find ways to thread film through their pinhole cameras and take actual photos.

Straw Flute

In Jesus' day, people played instruments when they mourned the dead. A drinking straw is all you need to make your own instrument.

Do It

1. Flatten about an inch of one end of the straw using your front teeth (if you have them!) or your thumb and forefinger.

2. Cut two narrow triangles from the sides of the flattened end so you have a V shape. Leave a slightly blunt tip.

3. Put about two inches of the V-shaped end into your mouth.

4. Roll your lips inward and blow until you hear a "duck call" sound when you blow. If you don't hear it on the first attempt, try moving the straw in or out or blowing harder or more gently.

5. To vary the sound, cut the straw shorter. Or, make it longer: slit a second straw lengthwise with the scissors. Roll it tightly and insert it into the end of your straw. What sound can you make now?

Get It

Straws

Scissors

Hole punch (optional)

Try It!

Cut fingering holes into your instrument. Slightly crease your straw and position a hole punch over it so it uses only about a third of the punching-out circle. Punch through the two layers of straw so you have a circular hole (like cutting paper snowflakes). Make two or three holes along the length of the straw. Now play, covering and uncovering the holes to see what pitches you can make.

Understand It

You've just made a wind instrument. The vibration of the "reed" you cut into the straw causes a series of compression waves in the air that we hear as sound when the waves cause our eardrums to vibrate. Shortening or lengthening the straw changes the nature of the waves, raising and lowering the pitch that we hear. If you do this activity with friends, make instruments of varying lengths to produce the notes of a musical scale and play a song together.

Read It

Mark 5:21–43

How do you feel when you're waiting in a long line at a store or at the movies? Impatient, or even angry? Imagine poor Jairus, anxiously walking with Jesus while his daughter's life slipped away. Jesus was slowed by the crowds and then He stopped to talk with someone else who needed His healing. Jairus waited as the minutes slipped away. When he saw the solemn messengers approach, Jairus must have felt a jumble of emotions. He knew Jesus had the power to heal. He did not yet know that Jesus had power over death. But because he trusted Jesus, his mourning finally turned to joy when his daughter was restored to life. This miracle showed the people of the time that Jesus was God. It teaches us the same thing—that Jesus has power over our eternal enemies: death, sin, and the devil. We share in the same joy as Jairus!

Learn It

[Jesus said], "Do not fear, only believe."

Mark 5:36

Read It

Matthew 16:13–19

When he met Jesus, Peter, like John the Baptist, felt unworthy: "Depart from me, for I am a sinful man, O Lord" (Luke 5:8). From the very start, Peter knew that Jesus was the Messiah. Although he was a humble fisherman, he was not swayed by the opinions of others, even the opinions of educated religious leaders. Perhaps that's why Jesus changed Simon's name to Peter, which means "rock" (John 1:42). Many people today believe Jesus was just a good man. The Holy Spirit gives you faith so you can believe the Scriptures, which tell the truth about Jesus. Believe as Peter did!

Learn It

[Jesus] said to them, "But who do you say that I am?" Simon Peter replied, "You are the Christ, the Son of the living God." And Jesus answered him, "Blessed are you, Simon Bar-Jonah! For flesh and blood has not revealed this to you, but My Father who is in heaven."

Matthew 16:15–17

Wobbly Bones

People's views on Jesus' identity were a little wobbly, but Peter had backbone. Do you think bones can be made to wobble?

Do It

1. After you've had a chicken or turkey dinner, remove some of the thinner bones (wishbone, leg, or wing bones) from the cooked carcass, wash them, and let them dry.

2. Put the bones in a jar of vinegar and screw on the lid.

3. Let the bones sit for a few days. Once in a while, take the bones out of the jar. What do they feel like?

Understand It

Vinegar is a mild acid that dissolves the calcium and other hard minerals in the bones, leaving behind only the soft part of the bone, which is a protein called collagen. You can bend the bones and they won't break!

Get It

Clean chicken or turkey bones

Vinegar

Quart jar with lid

Sidewalk Chalk

Jesus wrote in the dust with His finger. You can make your own sidewalk chalk.

Do It

1. Cut a toilet paper roll from top to bottom and roll up tightly. Secure with tape. Cover the bottom of one end with several pieces of tape.

2. Cut a strip of waxed paper as tall as the toilet paper roll and roll it up. Slip it inside the toilet paper roll.

3. Put ¼ cup of water in the cup. Measure ½ cup of the plaster of paris and add it one spoonful at a time to the cup, stirring to mix. It should become like a batter.

4. Add one spoonful of liquid or powder tempura paint and mix well.

5. Holding your toilet paper roll upright, pour the mixture (or drop by spoonfuls) into the roll. Tap the sides of the roll to release any air bubbles and prop the roll upright in a box or jar. Let it dry overnight.

6. Unwrap the chalk and let it dry completely before you use it.

Get It

- Scissors
- Toilet paper roll
- Packing tape
- Waxed paper
- Plastic cup
- Measuring cups
- Water
- Plaster of paris
- Plastic spoon
- Tempura paint
- Jar or box

Understand It

Blackboard or sidewalk chalk is made from a mineral called gypsum (calcium sulfate). It crumbles easily, leaving particles that stick loosely to a surface. Plaster of paris, a building material, is a mixture of powdered and heat-treated gypsum. When it is mixed with water, plaster of paris hardens to a smooth solid that does not shrink or lose volume because it hardens before all the water can evaporate.

A Woman Is Forgiven

Read It

John 8:1–11

What was Jesus writing in the dust? Like many stories in the Bible, this one is brief and doesn't give many details. We don't know what He was writing or why. Instead, we need to focus on the message of this story. A woman had sinned and was going to be killed, according to Jewish law. Jesus challenged those who had judged her to carry out the sentence only if they themselves had never sinned. And, of course, no one but Jesus has ever lived a sinless life. Jesus forgave this woman and He forgives us. However, there are consequences of sin. Someone who cheats on a test may have to take a failing grade, for example. Yet Jesus wants us to be merciful toward others and not be quick to judge their motives and actions. He took the punishment for this woman's sin—and for all of our sins—when He suffered and died on the cross. We are forgiven and God is merciful to us. We can forgive others because we are forgiven.

Learn It

[Jesus] stood up and said to them, "Let him who is without sin among you be the first to throw a stone at her."

John 8:7

It's History

In the 1700s, the walls of wooden houses in Paris were covered with plaster to protect them from fire. It became a common practice in the city after a fire nearly destroyed London in 1666. Gypsum deposits were plentiful in areas outside the city, hence the name plaster of paris.

A Visit from Jesus

Read It

Luke 10:38–42

What goes on at your house when company is coming? Most likely a flurry of cooking and cleaning. We do this to show guests they are welcomed and wanted. Martha wanted to welcome Jesus with a clean home and a good meal. That wasn't wrong. But could you imagine ignoring Jesus today while you stuff the turkey and run the vacuum? Yet we do that all time when we fill our days with activity and forget to take the time to read the Bible and learn from God's Word. To Martha, her sister, Mary, seemed lazy, but Jesus was pleased with Mary's stillness and her desire to learn from Him. We can do the same today. When we go to church or have daily devotions, we can clear our hearts and minds of sinful thoughts in preparation for hearing the Gospel of Jesus Christ.

Learn It

But the Lord answered her, "Martha, Martha, you are anxious and troubled about many things, but one thing is necessary. Mary has chosen the good portion, which will not be taken away from her." **Luke 10:41–42**

Fading Fur

Martha wanted to make her home a welcome place for Jesus. Here's a fun way to clean up!

Do It

1. Fill the jar ¾ full with bleach.
2. Use the spoon to carefully push the fur down into the bleach.
3. Watch what happens!

Understand It

The fur dissolves almost instantly! Bleach is an acid, and fur (or feathers and hair) is a base. Combining the two produces a chemical reaction. The bleach releases oxygen when it comes in contact with the hair—you see foam and bubbles on the surface—and, then, voila! What a way to clean up!

Note: Protect your eyes and wear old clothes—spilled bleach may burn your skin and take the color out of your clothes.

Get It

- Small jars with lids (baby food or jam jars)
- Liquid bleach
- Dog or cat fur, human hair, or bird feathers
- rubber gloves
- disposable spoon (plastic)
- protective eye goggles

CAUTION!

Handle bleach with care. Avoid contact with skin and eyes. Avoid inhaling.

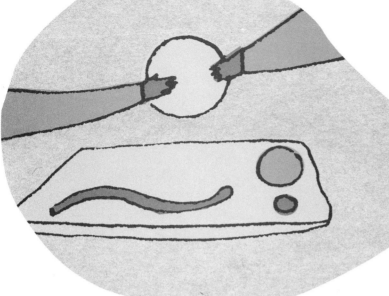

Clay Dough

Jesus used mud to heal a blind man's eyes. This mud can't heal, but it smells good and it's fun to play with.

Do It

1. In a medium size pot, mix 1 cup of flour, ¼ cup of salt, 2 tablespoons cream of tartar, and one package of unsweetened flavored drink powder in any color you'd like.

2. Pour in 1 tablespoon vegetable oil and 1 cup of water. Put the pot on the stovetop over medium heat. Stir the mixture as it heats.

3. In about 5 minutes, the mixture will begin to take a solid shape. Turn the dough out onto a cutting board and knead until it is smooth.

4. The dough can be made with food coloring instead of flavored drink powder. Add the food coloring after you've turned the dough out onto the board. Knead in color. You can also divide the dough and knead in different colors.

Get It

- Pot
- Measuring cups and spoons
- Flour
- Salt
- Cream of tartar
- Flavored drink powder
- Vegetable oil
- Water
- Cutting board

Understand It

In any recipe, heat can be thought of as another ingredient: it is a form of energy that changes the nature of these separate ingredients— liquids and solids—so they combine into a single solid. The flour contains a protein called gluten, which makes the dough stick together. To use the clay dough again, keep it in an airtight container. Otherwise, mold it into a shape you like and let it air-dry.

Read It

John 9

With mud covering his eyes, this man, blind from birth, made his way to a pool of water. Do you think maybe he felt a little odd walking past people with mud on his face? Perhaps because of his disability he had already grown used to rude comments from bystanders. But because he did what Jesus said to do, he was given his sight. He quickly came to believe that Jesus was from God, and he stood firm in his belief because of what Jesus had done for him, even when the Pharisees questioned and rejected him. This man received the gift of faith in Jesus, the Son of God. We have the same faith. We received it through the waters of Holy Baptism and the Word of God. The Holy Spirit keeps us in this faith. Stand firm in your belief no matter what others might be thinking or saying about you or about Jesus.

Learn It

"One thing I do know, that though I was blind, now I see. ... Never since the world began has it been heard that anyone opened the eyes of a man born blind. If this man were not from God, he could do nothing."

John 9:25, 32–33

A Woman's Deed Is Praised

Read It

Matthew 26:6–13

Suppose you saved all of your birthday and Christmas money to buy an expensive video game or computer game. How easy would it be to just give the game away? The woman in this story took something of hers, a jar of perfume that cost a lot of money, and poured it on Jesus' head. This was her way of showing that she loved and honored Jesus. Others condemned her act as a waste of money, but Jesus saw it as an act of deep devotion. He praised the woman and rewarded her with an honored place in Christian history. Jesus gave something very valuable to us: His life on a cross. Don't hold back your gifts from God. "For God loves a cheerful giver" (2 Corinthians 9:7). What are some ways you can give back to God?

Learn It

[Jesus] said to them, "Why do you trouble the woman? For she has done a beautiful thing to Me. For you always have the poor with you, but you will not always have Me. In pouring this ointment on My body, she has done it to prepare Me for burial. Truly, I say to you, wherever this gospel is proclaimed in the whole world, what she has done will also be told in memory of her."

Matthew 26:10–13

Spicy Scents

This woman used perfume to show her devotion to Jesus. We can make a sweet-smelling perfume from simple spices.

Do It

1. Fill the jars 3/4 full with rubbing alcohol.

2. Drop in fifteen or twenty whole spices. Experiment with one spice per jar or any combination you wish. Cap the jars.

3. Let the perfume sit for a week.

4. Open the jars and dab the perfume on your wrist. Take a whiff.

Get It

Small jars with lids (baby food jars or small jam jars)

Rubbing alcohol

Whole spices (cloves, star anise, cinnamon stick, allspice, etc.)

Understand It

The alcohol dissolves the aromatic oil of the spices. When the alcohol evaporates from your wrist, the scented oil is left behind on your skin. Perfumes and colognes are made this way, by dissolving flowers, spices, and other pleasant-smelling ingredients in alcohol.

Caught Up with Excitement

Swirling Whirls

People were caught up in a whirl of emotion when Jesus rode into Jerusalem. Watch the whirls and swirls of this soap-and-water mixture.

Get It

Round mason or jelly jar, or bottle with lid

Liquid soap

Food coloring

Water

Do It

1. Using a soap that contains glycerin or glycol stearate, squeeze out liquid soap into a round jar until it is about a quarter full. (Round bottles with a neck work well, too, since you can hold them easily.)

2. Squeeze in a few drops of red or yellow food coloring. Don't mix the drops into the soap.

3. Run a trickle of water from a faucet. Fill the jar to the top, letting the water run down the inside of the jar to avoid making foam. If you do get foam, simply run the water over the top of the jar and let the foam rinse away.

4. Put lid on tightly. Turn the jar upside down a few times to combine the soap and water. Then, move the jar in any way you like. Flip it upside down, twirl it, spin it one way and then in reverse. Hold it up to the light to see the motion better.

Understand It

Glycerin or glycol stearate, an ingredient in many hand soaps, is made from animal and plant fats. It is used to add texture and a pearly, opaque look. Here, it allows you to see the motion of liquids. Watch the food coloring as it whirls around in the soap and water solution and finally mixes in. (Add more drops of color if you want.) Then watch the opaque swirls of the soap itself.

Read It

Mark 11:1–11

The sound of applause feels great after you've played your recital piece. And the cheers of your friends and family are a welcome roar after you've scored a soccer goal. Jesus rode into Jerusalem in triumph, on the back of a donkey colt, just as the prophet Zechariah had said He would more than 500 years earlier (Zechariah 9:9). Many people had gathered in Jerusalem to celebrate the Jewish feast of Passover. People cheered and shouted, "Blessed is He who comes in the name of the Lord!" (Mark 11:9). They waved palm branches and laid their cloaks on the ground for Jesus. This was a big, happy celebration! Yet Jesus knew that in just a few days, when their hopes for an earthly king had been dashed, people would shout, "Crucify Him" (Mark 15:13). Today we observe this event as Palm Sunday, the beginning of Holy Week and Easter. Jesus did indeed triumph— over sin and death!

Learn It

And those who went before and those who followed were shouting, "Hosanna! Blessed is He who comes in the name of the Lord! Blessed is the coming kingdom of our father David! Hosanna in the highest!"

Mark 11:9–10

The Drumbeat of Time

Read It

Luke 21:5–38;
2 Corinthians 6:2

You depend on clocks throughout the day. They let you know when classes begin and end. They help you judge your speed on the track or in a pool. They tell you when dinner or bedtime is approaching. All of human history is measured with time. But Jesus taught that time will one day come to an end. When He comes back, time will no longer have any meaning. Eternity has no need of clocks. Jesus often spoke of the end of time, and in this passage in the Bible, He pleads with us to be ready for that eternal moment. He wants us all to receive His work of forgiveness and salvation on the cross so our eternity will be spent with Him.

Learn It

"For He says, 'In a favorable time I listened to you, and in a day of salvation I have helped you.' Behold, now is the favorable time; behold, now is the day of salvation."

2 Corinthians 6:2

Shrink Wrap Drum

The drumbeat of earthly time will someday end. Let's keep time with a set of homemade drums.

Do It

1. Wrap a piece of double-sided tape around the outside of a variety of metal mixing bowls, about one inch below the rims. (Nested bowls of graduated sizes work well.)

2. Stretch a piece of plastic wrap over the bowls and press it onto the tape. Overlap two pieces of wrap for very large bowls.

3. Start the blow dryer on high heat and blow over and around the bowls for a few seconds. The wrap should puff up and tighten around the bowls.

4. Using craft sticks or chopsticks, try out your drums. How do they sound? How does size affect sound? Do they sound better on a floor or table or if you hold them?

Get It

- Double-sided tape
- Metal bowls
- Plastic wrap
- Blow dryer
- Craft sticks or chopsticks

Understand It

Plastic wrap is made from long strands of molecules called polymers that are artificially stretched out. When you apply heat—a form of energy—the molecules get moving and return to their natural tangled state, which shrinks the wrap in size and increases its strength. That thin film makes a great drum!

Jesus Becomes a Servant

Sweaty Feet

Jesus took the humble job of washing dusty, dirty feet. It's not the sweetest smelling work, as you'll find out when you get a whiff of these socks.

Do It

1. Take off your sweaty socks after you've worn and played in them for a while.

2. Spritz them with water a few times, and then seal the socks in a plastic bag.

3. Put the bag in the sun to sit for a few hours or overnight.

4. Open the bag—if you dare!

Get It

Sweaty socks
Spray bottle
Water
Plastic bag

Understand It

It's the brave soul who opens this bag! Sweat is your body's way of cooling itself and keeping skin moist and flexible. One foot has more than 250,000 sweat glands! Sweat is basically a mix of salt and water and doesn't have a real odor of its own. The icky smell the bag releases is actually caused by bacteria on your skin that eat the sweat and excrete a stinky waste. The water and heat from the sun multiply the bacteria—and the odor!

Read It

John 13:1–20

When was the last time you volunteered to do the laundry for your family or clean the bathroom? Some household jobs are just no fun. Not only that, but they seem somehow beneath our dignity. By taking on a task that a servant would normally have done—washing the dirty, muddy feet of people who walked dusty roads all day long— Jesus set a powerful example for us. He teaches that acts of service to others, no matter how humble or lowly, are acts of devotion to God. Jesus' ultimate act of service was enduring the cross and dying for the sins of the world. Thinking of this Bible story encourages us to serve others willingly.

Learn It

[Jesus said,] "Truly, truly, I say to you, a servant is not greater than his master, nor is a messenger greater than the one who sent him. If you know these things, blessed are you if you do them."

John 13:16–17

God Grants Earthly Power

Read It

John 18:28–19:22

Sometimes it seems that everyone in the world has power over you—parents, teachers, coaches. They say "do this" or "do that," and you have to obey. In reality, any power adults have is granted by God, and they should use it to glorify Him and help you gain knowledge, maturity, and wisdom. By obeying them, you obey God. Even at His trial, Jesus taught this lesson to Pilate, who thought he held power over Jesus' death. But God was in control. He allowed Pilate to use his authority to bring about Jesus' death and resurrection for our salvation. Jesus' death was all part of God's great plan to provide us with forgiveness for our sins.

Learn It

Jesus answered him, "You would have no authority over Me at all unless it had been given you from above."

John 19:11

Lemon Battery

Jesus told Pilate that it is God who grants power. Without a light switch or a battery, we can make a tiny jolt of power.

Get It

Lemon
Knife
Penny
Dime

Do It

1. Roll the lemon on a counter, pressing down with your palms. (This breaks the inner membranes and releases the juice.)

2. Cut two small slits in the lemon peel, into the juicy part, about ½-inch apart. Put the penny in one slot and the dime in the other.

3. Stick out your tongue and place it between the two coins, touching both at the same time. What can you feel?

Understand It

You've made a battery! A battery produces electricity, which is the flow of electrons through a conductive path. It is made of an anode (a negative charge), a cathode (a positive charge), an electrolyte that starts the process through a chemical reaction, and a connector (usually a wire) that conducts the electrical current. Here, the zinc in the dime is the anode, the copper of the penny is the cathode, and the citric acid in the lemon is the electrolyte. Your tongue completes the circuit, causing a tingling sensation and a metallic taste as the current passes through it.

A Thief Believes

Floating Drop

Suspended between life and death on a cross, one thief believed in Jesus. We can make drops of oil look suspended in midair.

Get It

Clear drinking glass
Water
Rubbing alcohol
Cooking oil
Medicine dropper

Do It

1. Fill the glass half-full with water.

2. Tilt the glass slightly, and slowly pour in rubbing alcohol so it runs down the inside of the glass. Keep pouring until the glass is almost full and then carefully set the glass on a tabletop or counter.

3. Fill a medicine dropper with oil and lower the tip into the layer of rubbing alcohol. Squeeze out some drops. Where do they end up?

Understand It

Rubbing alcohol is slightly less dense than water, so it remains on top of the water if added carefully. (The two liquids will mix if shaken.) Oil is less dense than water but more dense than rubbing alcohol, so the oil drops remain suspended between the two liquids.

Read It

Luke 23:32–43

Imagine being so hard-hearted that even as your life slipped away, you mocked God. Yet that's what one thief did as he died on a cross next to Jesus. The other thief saw eternity approaching and seized the opportunity to ask for God's mercy. The promise that he would that very day be with Jesus in heaven must have helped him endure his suffering. Don't let your heart become too hard to believe in Jesus' saving work on the cross. "A broken and contrite heart, O God, You will not despise" (Psalm 51:17).

Learn It

"We are receiving the due reward of our deeds; but this man has done nothing wrong. . . . Jesus, remember me when You come into Your kingdom." And He said to him, "Truly, I say to you, today you will be with Me in Paradise."

Luke 23:41–43

Stephen's Final Words

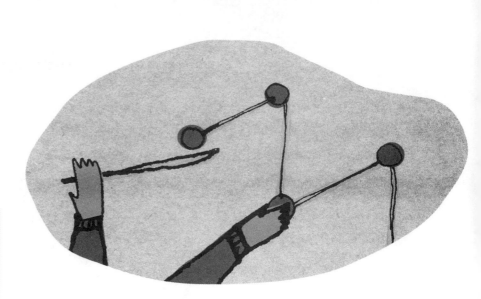

Read It

Acts 7

Do you do some things because you think somehow they will earn you God's approval? Go to church each Sunday? Give a certain amount of money or say the right prayers? But Stephen preached that there are no religious activities by which we earn God's favor. "You stiff-necked people, uncircumcised in heart and ears, you always resist the Holy Spirit," he told the Jewish leaders, who wanted to maintain their worthless rules and rituals (Acts 7:51). How do you earn God's approval? It's simple: you don't. Only Jesus can do that for you. By giving His life on your behalf, He provided a way for all your sins to be forgiven and to receive God's grace. Now, when God looks at you, He sees the righteousness that Jesus earned for you.

Learn It

"Heaven is My throne, and the earth is My footstool. What kind of house will you build for Me, says the Lord, or what is the place of My rest? Did not My hand make all these things?"

Acts 7:49–50

Pea Construction

God's Church is the body of believers, a Church that is built up every time someone is brought to faith. Let's see what we can build with toothpicks and peas.

Do It

1. Cover the peas or beans with water in a bowl and soak them overnight. They are ready when you can pierce them with a toothpick. Leave them in water while you work, so they remain soft.

2. Make a structure by piercing the peas with the toothpicks. (Gumdrops—although sticky!—might be easier for young children to handle.)

3. Try forming different shapes (squares, triangles) and note which shapes make your structure more, or less, stable.

Understand It

Did you find that triangles make the strongest structures? The angles of a triangle cannot change once the triangle has been built: a triangle has three sides and three angles, and each angle is fixed by the side opposite it. Squares and rectangles are wobbly—you can easily change their angles. Architects often use triangular shapes to make buildings and bridges strong.

Get It

Bowl

Whole peas, pigeon peas or other round pea or bean (or gumdrops)

Water

Wooden toothpicks

Try It!

Construct a geodesic dome by connecting triangles into a sphere. Start with a flat, five-sided base of toothpicks and beans or gumdrops. Start building triangles up until you can connect all the toothpick points at the top with one bean. Because of its triangular elements, a geodesic dome gets stronger the larger it is built.

3-D Glasses

Paul was blinded for three days after his encounter with the risen Lord. Glasses would not have helped him see, but let's see what they can do for us.

Do It

1. Cut out the pattern for 3-D glasses on page 63. Place the pattern over card stock or cardboard, trace it, and then cut out the glasses.

2. From the cellophane bags, cut out eye holes to fit the glasses, one of red and one of blue. Cut from the sides of the bags, where the cellophane has four layers, or cut two double layers from the center of the bag. (Party stores or candy-making supply stores carry these bags.)

3. Tape the cellophane cutouts to the eyeholes, red on the left eye and blue on the right. You can cut out a second cardboard pattern and glue it over the first to make sturdier glasses. Tape the ear pieces to the sides of the glasses.

4. Obtain 3-D images from a website with an image gallery. Wear your glasses to view them on the computer screen or a color printout.

Get It

- Scissors
- Card stock or cardboard
- Pencil
- Cellophane gift bags (red and blue)
- Tape
- Glue

Understand It

The pictures jump off the page! Your eyes are a few inches apart and view objects from slightly different angles. In a process called binocular vision, your brain puts these two images together and gauges distances. In a 3D photo, the same scene is shown from two different angles in red and blue. The colored cellophane separates the two images so each image enters only one eye. This tricks the brain into putting the two pictures back together in an astonishing way.

Read It

Acts 9:1–20, 22:1–16

Saul had an eye-popping experience! He was on his way to capture Christians and force them back to Jerusalem in chains when a blinding light stopped him in his tracks. It was none other than the risen Christ! Jesus asked a very direct question: Why was Saul persecuting Him? He didn't ask why he was persecuting the Christians. In His ministry, Jesus said, "Truly, I say to you, as you did it to one of the least of these My brothers, you did it to Me" (Matthew 25:40). We show our love (or lack of it) for Jesus by how we treat other people. Because Jesus loved us first, we can love others. Saul got the message—he is known to us today as the apostle Paul, the great champion of Christ who brought countless others to faith.

Learn It

And he said, "The God of our fathers appointed you to know His will, to see the Righteous One and to hear a voice from His mouth; for you will be a witness for Him to everyone of what you have seen and heard. And now why do you wait? Rise and be baptized and wash away your sins, calling on His name."

Acts 22:14–16

Read It

Acts 10

Some people think the world is so large and filled with so many people that God couldn't possibly have enough time to listen to or care about them. Do you ever wonder whether God hears your prayers or cares what you do? Cornelius was a kind man who feared God, even before he knew about or believed in Jesus. God sent an angel to Cornelius to say, "Your prayers and your alms have ascended as a memorial before God" (Acts 10:4). God arranged things so Cornelius could meet Peter, who taught him that the message of the Gospel of Jesus Christ is for all people, not just for a few. Then Cornelius and the others at his home who heard Peter preach were baptized in Jesus' name. God hears your prayers too. And God sends pastors to us to preach His Word and administer the sacraments of Baptism and the Lord's Supper to bring us to faith.

Learn It

In every nation anyone who fears Him and does what is right is acceptable to Him. As for the word that He sent to Israel, preaching good news of peace through Jesus Christ (He is Lord of all).

Acts 10:35–36

It's History

Hundreds of years before Christ, builders in ancient civilizations such as the Etruscans and Romans understood this idea and used it to construct buildings, bridges, and aqueducts.

Egg Bridge

Through Christ, we have a bridge of peace to God. Who would think you can make a bridge out of something as fragile as eggshells?

Get It

4 raw eggs, in their shells

Scissors

Books or videos

Do It

1. Using the point of the scissors, poke a hole in the small end of the egg. With your fingers, tear away a small hole and pour the egg out. Rinse the shell gently, inside and out, and wipe the outside dry.

2. From the hole, make cuts with the scissors toward the middle of the shell, as you would score an orange to peel it. Peel away the scored shell in small bits, until you have a dome-shaped half-shell.

3. Repeat steps 1 and 2 until you have four eggshell domes of the same height. Space them out on a table or counter so they form a support for the corners of your books or videos.

4. Begin to pile your books or videos onto the egg domes. How many will your egg "bridge" support?

Understand It

Can you believe the weight your egg domes supported? Domes and arches—even when made from fragile eggshells—are strong because they exert horizontal and vertical forces that resist the pressure of heavy loads. The crown of an eggshell can support far more weight than you'd imagine because it evenly distributes it around the shell.

An Eternity of Praise

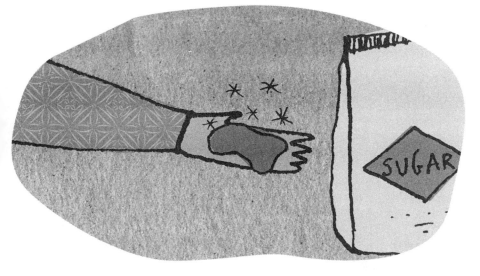

Sugar Glass Sea

In his vision, John saw a sea of glass in front of the throne of God, sparkling like crystal. Let's make a crystal-clear sea of sugar glass.

Get It

- Baking sheet
- Aluminum foil
- Measuring cup
- Sugar
- Frying pan
- Food coloring
- Wooden spoon

Do It

1. Line a baking sheet with aluminum foil.

2. Pour 1 cup of sugar into a frying pan. Add a few drops of food coloring.

3. Put the frying pan on a stovetop and slowly melt the sugar on medium heat, stirring all the time. This will take a while. The sugar will form hard clumps, and then melt into a liquid. Be very careful—the sugar is very hot at this point.

4. Have an adult pour the sugar onto the baking sheet—it is scalding hot. Spread the sugar out with the back of a spoon. Put the sheet in a refrigerator.

5. When the sugar has cooled and hardened, take the baking sheet out of the refrigerator and peel the foil from the back of the sugar "sea."

Understand It

Sugar is made up of crystals whose molecules break apart when heated and melt into a syrup. The molecules reconnect as the syrup cools, forming a solid sheet of sugar "glass." Real glass is made from soda, lime, and sand, which has crystals just as sugar does. Glass can be as strong as a fish tank or as delicate as a Christmas ornament.

Read It

Revelation 4–5

If you could see into the future, would you want to? Maybe you'd want to know whether you passed that math test, or won that big game, or got invited to that special party. God gave John, the writer of the Book of Revelation, a vision of our future life in heaven. It was an astonishing vision, one whose details we could discuss endlessly. But the big picture of the future is this: When God says that it is time, all creatures in heaven and on earth will give praise and honor to God the Father, God the Son, and God the Holy Spirit.

Learn It

And the four living creatures, each of them with six wings, are full of eyes all around and within, and day and night they never cease to say, "Holy, holy, holy, is the Lord God Almighty, who was and is and is to come! . . . Worthy are You, our Lord and God, to receive glory and honor and power, for You created all things, and by Your will they existed and were created."

Revelation 4:8, 11

List of Materials

You will not need all of these materials. Some activities can be set up with alternate materials that are listed here along with the primary materials.

Nonperishables

Adding machine paper

Aluminum foil

Ammonia

Art brushes

Baking sheet

Balloons

Bleach (all-fabric powder)

Bleach (chlorine)

Blow dryer

Borax (powdered)

Bottle (glass)

Bowls (mixing)

Box (small cardboard)

Bubble-blowing liquid

Bubble wands

Buttons

Cardboard

Card stock

Cellophane gift bags
(red and blue)

Cereal bowl

Chenille wires

Chopsticks

Cloth (white)

Coffee can

Coffee filters

Coins (dime, penny)

Construction paper
(white and dark)

Correction fluid

Cotton balls

Cotton swabs

Cups (paper and plastic)

Dish detergent

Dishes

Dowel

Drinking glass (clear)

Drinking straws (plastic)

Fluorescent light bulb

Garbage bag (black plastic)

Gloves

Glue

Glycerin

Hole punch

Inked pad

Jars (all sizes)

Juice carton (empty)

Knives (sharp and plastic)

Lunch box

Medicine dropper

Newspaper

Notepad

Markers

Matches

Measuring cups

Measuring spoons

Mirrors (wall and hand)

Pans (baking, frying)

Paper (white)

Paper clips

Paper plates

Paper towel rolls (empty)

Paper towels

Peanut butter jar (empty)

Pencils (regular and colored)

Plaster of paris

Plastic bags
(regular and freezer)

Plastic wrap

Craft sticks

Potato chip tube

Potholders

Rolling pin

Rubbing alcohol

Ruler

Sand (craft)

Saucepan

Saucer

Scissors

Soap (liquid)

Socks

Soda bottles (1- or 2-liter)

Spoons (all kinds)

Spray bottle

Stamps (inked)

Stencils

Strainer

String

Styrofoam tray

Tape (masking, Scotch,
packing, double-sided)

Telephone books

Tempera paint

3 × 5 cards

Thumbtack

Toilet paper rolls (empty)

Toothbrush

Towels

Twist ties

Washing soda

Waxed paper

Whisk

Wool (fabric or sweater)

Perishables

Antacid tablets

Apple

Baking soda

Bones (chicken or turkey)

Cabbage (red)

Cola, diet

Cooking oil

Cream (heavy)

Cream of tartar

Eggs

Flavored oils (or extracts)

Flour

Food coloring

Fur (or feathers or hair)

Gelatin (flavored and unflavored)

Grape juice (purple)

Gumdrops

Ice cubes

Flavored drink powder

Leaves (deciduous)

Lemon

Lemon juice

Mentos® candy

Milk (fresh and powdered)

Nail polish (clear)

Peas (dry whole or pigeon peas)

Salt

Spices (whole)

Sugar

Vanilla extract

Vinegar (white)

Water

Scripture Index

Science Index

Selected Bibliography

Books

Buttitta, Hope. *It's Not Magic, It's Science! 50 Science Tricks that Mystify, Dazzle & Astound!* Asheville, NC: Lark Books, 2005.

Churchill, E. Richard. *365 Simple Science Experiments with Everyday Materials.* New York: Black Dog & Leventhal Publishers, 1997.

Kennedy, Nancy B. *Even the Sound Waves Obey Him.* St. Louis, MO: Concordia Publishing House, 2005.

Perry, Phyllis. *365 Science Projects & Activities.* Lincolnwood, Ill.: Publications International, 1997.

Penrose, Gordon. *Science Fun: Hands-On Science with Dr. Zed.* Toronto: Greey de Pencier Books, 1998.

Penrose, Gordon. *More Science Surprises from Dr. Zed.* Toronto: Maple Tree Press, 2002.

Robinson, Tom. *The Everything Kids' Science Experiments Book: Boil Ice, Float Water, Measure Gravity—Challenge the World Around You!* Cincinnati, OH: Adams Media, 2001.

Web Sites

About.com (www.about.com). Click on *Homework Help; Chemistry; Chemistry for Kids.*

American Paper Optics (www.3dglassesonline.com). 3D viewing photos. Click on *3D image gallery.*

Creative Kids at Home (www.creativekidsathome.com). Crafts, games and science activities. Click on *Kids Activity Library.*

The Exploratorium (www.exploratorium.edu). Museum of Science, Art, and Human Perception in San Francisco, California.

HowStuffWorks (www.howstuffworks.com). Click on *Science Stuff; Browse the Science Library,* or type a phrase into the Search field.

National Geographic Kids magazine (www.nationalgeographic.com/ngkids). Click on *Activities, Experiments.*

PBS Kids (www.pbskids.org/zoom). Based on PBS's ZOOM science show. Click on *Activities from the Show.*

Science Toy Maker (www.sciencetoymaker.org). Easy, well-tested activities that produce toys and objects.

Scitoys (www.sci-toys.com). Science activities and catalog of kits and equipment.

Teachnet (www.teachnet.com). Lesson plans and activities for classrooms. Click on *Lesson Plans, Science.*

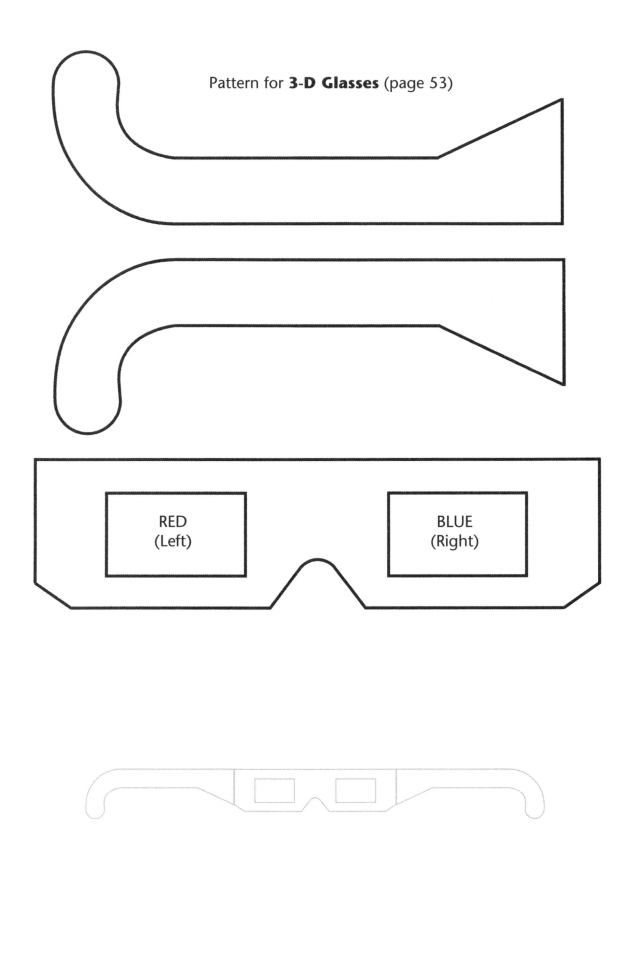

Pattern for **3-D Glasses** (page 53)

RED
(Left)

BLUE
(Right)